KNOW YOUR SPORT

Trampolining

Paul Mason

SEA-TO-SEA
Mankato Collingwood London

This edition first published in 2010 by
Sea-to-Sea Publications
Distributed by Black Rabbit Books
P.O. Box 3263, Mankato, Minnesota
56002

Printed in USA

Library of Congress Cataloging-in-Publication Data

Mason, Paul, 1967-
Trampolining / Paul Mason.
p. cm. -- (Know your sport)
Includes index.
ISBN 978-1-59771-219-4 (hardcover)
1. Trampolining. I. Title.
GV555.M37 2010
796.47--dc22
2008045864

9 8 7 6 5 4 3 2

Published by arrangement with the Watts Publishing Group Ltd., London

Series editor: Jeremy Smith
Art director: Jonathan Hair

Series designed and created for Franklin Watts by Storeybooks.
Designer: Rita Storey
Editor: Nicola Edwards
Photography: Tudor Photography, Banbury

Note: At the time of going to press, the statistics and player profiles in this book were up to date. However, due to some players' active participation in the sport, it is possible that some of these may now be out of date.

Picture credits

Alan Edwards pp 17 and 26; Getty Images p8; Bongarts/Getty Images p26; © Juan Vrijdag /epa/Corbis p20.

Cover images: Tudor Photography, Banbury.

All photos posed by models.
Thanks to Andrea Blake, Katie Emmings, Chris Lloyd, and Emma Trafford.

The Publisher would like to thank Airtime Trampoline Club, Gosford Hill School,and coach Nic Silversides for their help

WARNING: This book is not a substitute for learning from a skilled coach, which is the only safe way to learn trampolining techniques.

Taking part in a sport is a fun way to get in shape, but like any form of physical exercise it has an element of risk, particularly if you are unfit, overweight, or suffer from any medical conditions. It is advisable to consult a healthcare professional before beginning any program of exercise.

Contents

What is Trampolining?

Welcome to the high-flying, gymnastic world of trampolining. Trampolining is one of the newest Olympic sports, as well as being a popular backyard activity for tens of thousands of people around the world.

A Young Sport

The first modern trampolines were built in 1936 by George Nissen and Larry Griswold. Nissen was a gymnast and diver, and Griswold was a tumbler. They had seen how circus trapeze artists used the safety net to bounce back up and add extra tricks to their performances. They stretched a piece of canvas across an iron frame and joined it to the frame with strong springs. The trampoline was born.

Early Days

After World War II (1939–45), a craze for trampolines meant that many people tried one out. Some of them never had another try, but many became more skilled at trampolining. People soon got bored of just bouncing up and down, and began to do flips and twists. Gymnasts found trampolines useful for learning new aerial techniques. By the 1960s had arrived, trampolining had become recognized as a new sport.

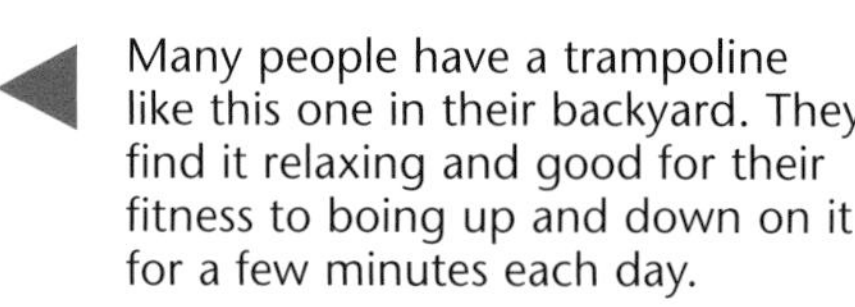

Many people have a trampoline like this one in their backyard. They find it relaxing and good for their fitness to boing up and down on it for a few minutes each day.

A trampolinist performing a somersault, a difficult skill that requires a lot of training.

Competition Trampolining

The first individual trampolining competitions were held in colleges and schools in the USA and then in Europe, with the first World Championships being held in London, England in 1964. Both winners, Dan Millman and Judy Wills Cline, were American. The USA went on to dominate the sport for many years to come. Other strong trampolining countries include the UK, France, Germany, Russia, and Canada. In 2000, trampolining was part of the Olympics for the first time. Russia won both the individual gold medals.

Trampolining and Other Sports

Trampolines are also used to train people for other sports and activities. These include diving, snowboarding, freestyle skiing, water skiing, and wrestling. Trampolines have even been used to train astronauts for weightlessness in space.

Trampolining Fact—or Fiction?

Circus people sometimes claim that a performer called du Trampolin invented modern trampolines. There's no evidence that such a person existed, though.

Trampolining Equipment

You don't need special clothing or shoes to start trampolining, which at heart is a simple sport. But trampolining can be dangerous, so it's important that the equipment you use is safe and well looked after.

The Trampoline

A trampoline is simply a piece of webbed fabric called a bed, attached to a strong frame using metal springs. If any of these breaks, the trampolinist can be seriously injured. Competition trampolines are made to a high standard, but cheap trampolines in people's backyards may not be. If you are in doubt about the quality of the trampoline, don't bounce on it.

Alexander Moskalenko

Date of birth: November 4th, 1969

Nationality: Russian

Moskalenko's place in the trampolining history books is assured. In 2000, he became the first Olympic trampolining champion ever. His other achievements include:

- **1990 world champion (despite breaking his back earlier in the year after a trampoline collapsed).**
- **1992 and 1994 world champion, after which he retired.**
- **Came back from retirement aiming to win Olympic gold. Became 1999 world champion, then won the 2000 Sydney Olympics easily.**
- **Silver medal at 2004 Athens Olympics.**

Alexander Moskaleko, known as the "King of Trampoline" because he was so rarely beaten in big competitions, on his way to silver at the 2004 Olympic Games.

Safety pads cover steel springs and frame.

bed

Like all proper clubs, this one has safety equipment to help prevent the trampolinists from injuring themselves during training.

Mats pushed in around side of trampoline.

Spotters ready to stop trampolinist from falling off.

Coach watches activity.

Safety Equipment

The trampoline mat should be surrounded by pads that cover the frame and springs. These make it impossible to land on them and bash yourself if you land badly. The trampoline itself should be impossible to topple over if you land on the pads. Many people put extra pads on the floor around the trampoline, in case the trampolinist bounces off or misses the mat altogether. As an alternative safety feature, some trampolines are enclosed in up-and-down netting, which makes it impossible for you to hit the ground.

Clothing and Footwear

Trampolining clothing needs to be comfortable and either loose (but not flappy) or stretchy, so that it's easy to move freely. Beginners usually wear long-sleeved tops and long leggings, to give their elbows and knees a bit of protection. Always wear socks or special trampolining shoes, so that there is less risk of your toes going through the webbing and being broken.

This trampolinist is using a "judo belt" during training. The belt is useful while practicing single somersaults. The coach stands on the bed and uses the belt to help the trampolinist control the somersault.

Training and Safety

Warming up before a trampolining session. Warming up is important, because it helps stop you from getting injuries during the twists and turns of a trampolining session.

If you have already tried trampolining and are now dreaming of doing spectacular high leaps, twists, and spins, you need to join a club. Clubs have qualified coaches who can help make your dreams come true.

Fitness

Most physically active people can take part in trampolining. It helps to be in reasonably good shape and flexible. If you aren't already, though, trampolining will help you to get that way. It helps build up strong muscles throughout the body. Trampolining is also good for improving your coordination and spatial awareness (the ability to know without thinking what shape and space your body is in).

Bouncing Sports

Trampolines are used in the sports of Slamball and Bossaball, which are versions of basketball and volleyball. They make a slam-dunk or a spike much easier!

Trampoline Safety

Trampolining is safe and fun if you follow these basic rules. If you don't, it can be extremely dangerous.

- A qualified supervisor, ideally a trampolining coach, should be watching at all times. Make sure this person knows of any medical conditions you have.
- The trampoline must be put together by someone who knows exactly what they are doing.
- Never swing on the end decks, or go underneath them or the trampoline itself.
- Always wear trampolining shoes or socks.
- Never trampoline for more than a minute at a time. Tiredness can lead to mistakes, so it's better to rest and then take another turn.
- Spotters (see page 9) must watch the trampolinist, and must not chat with each other or their friends nearby.
- When you leave the bed, be careful not to trip on the mats. Get down facing inward, toward the trampoline.

Coaching

The most important person to help you develop your trampolining ability is your coach. He or she will make sure that you learn new skills at the right speed. First you learn basic skills, such as bouncing in the middle of the bed and swinging your arms to gain height. Only when these are perfect should the coach let you go on to make shapes as you fly up and down through the air.

Coaches do a vital job in trampolining. Without a good coach and the right equipment, learning new skills properly is almost impossible.

Basic Technique

The basic technique of trampolining is to jump up and down smoothly. Experts are able to decide how high to jump, and add turns while making a variety of shapes with their bodies.

The Neutral Position

This is the position from which all trampolining moves start. Trampolinists are in the neutral position when they land dead center in the middle of the bed, and the bed has stretched downward as far as it will go.

Basic Phases

1 *In the neutral position the trampolinist has slightly bent legs and has sunk right into the bed. A beginner's arms would be above her head, but experts use an arm swing.*

2 *This is the transition from takeoff to flight, just as the trampolinist's feet leave the bed. Her knees, ankles, and feet are all stretched to make the most of the spring up from the bed.*

3 *Midway through the flight, the trampolinist is at her maximum height. Experienced trampolinists use an arm swing to get added power and height in their flight, but beginners do not need this and keep their arms above their head the whole time.*

Basic Elements

Every trampolining move is made up of three basic phases:

1) Takeoff

This is the phase between the neutral position and the moment when the trampolinist's feet leave the bed.

2) Flight

This is the phase between the moment the trampolinist's feet leave the bed and when they first touch it again.

3) Landing

"Landing" is the phase between the trampolinist's feet first touching the bed and the neutral position.

4 *The start of the landing phase, with the trampolinist's feet coming back into contact with the bed. At this point, her legs are straight—they only bend as the bed starts to sink down.*

Hitting the Bed

The ideal place for takeoff and landing is the dead center of the bed, which is marked with a cross. One of the first skills trampolinists have to learn is being able to take off and land from this exact spot time after time, without looking.

Stopping

Stopping is a basic trampolining skill. It means stopping the bounce of the bed, which trampolinists do using a deep knee bend just as their feet touch the bed at the start of the landing phase.

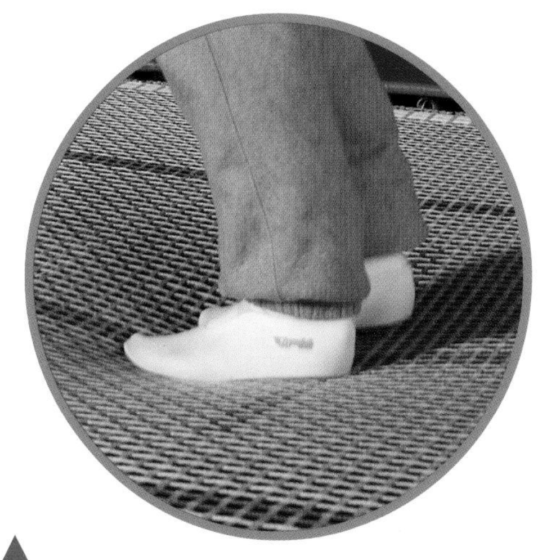

The bed of a trampoline has a cross on it that shows where its exact center is.

Watch out!

Always make sure you know where you are on the bed. Bouncing without being sure where your feet are landing is very dangerous.

The Takeoff

The takeoff phase is the one where the trampolinist prepares for the spectacular techniques that follow. Unless the takeoff is right, the flight phase will not work properly.

Types of Takeoff

There are two basic types of takeoff: foot and nonfoot ones. People who are new to trampolining start by learning foot takeoffs. There are four basic types of takeoff from your feet. Which you use depends on what you want to do during the flight phase:

1) No-rotation takeoffs are used for jumping straight up;
2) Forward and backward rotation takeoffs are used for rolls in the air;
3) Twist takeoffs are used for twists in the air;

A basic, straight takeoff position like this allows the trampolinist to jump straight in the air. For forward and backward rotations (tumbles), she would bend at the waist: forward to set up a forward rotation, backward to set up a backward one.

A seat takeoff. The trampolinist lands with straight legs, a bent waist, and arms out straight behind him, with his hands in contact with the bed.

4) takeoffs combining rotation and twist are used for techniques that combine the two.

Nonfoot takeoffs

Trampolinists don't just land and take off on their feet. Some techniques finish with a landing on the trampolinist's back, bottom, or front, so the trampolinist has to take off from these positions too. These alternate takeoffs are tricky and can be dangerous, so they should only be practiced with the help of a qualified coach. It is easy to lose height during a nonfoot landing, so they tend to be used by more advanced trampolinists.

The Arm Swing

To gain height, advanced gymnasts use an arm swing to add power to their bounce. Beginners don't need to use this, because it's more important to learn a safe, steady technique than to get as high as you can.

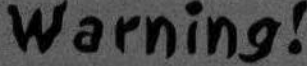

Try to avoid landing on your knees alone, because this can easily cause a back injury.

In a back takeoff, the trampolinist has her arms and legs pointing straight up in the air.

During a front takeoff like this one, the trampolinist holds her arms out to the side and bent forward at the elbow, making a diamond shape under her chin.

Flight 1—Basics

The flight phases are the most spectacular parts of a trampolining routine. It's during the flight phase that the trampolinist performs amazing twists and flips in the air.

Learning Skills

New trampolinists do not need to reach great heights to learn basic skills. Many of the basic skills and techniques they need can be practiced either from a "push and go" (a single deep bounce off the bed) or from three small bounces with no arm swing. Once they get to a more advanced stage, and are ready for competitions, this changes.

Straight Jump With Arm Swing

In a straight flight, the head, body, and legs are all in a straight line without any bend. The trampolinist's legs are together, and her toes, feet, and ankles are pointed.

1 *At the top of the flight stage, the trampolinist's arms are stretched upward.*

2 *On the way back down, the trampolinist's arms are coming down, still straight but now out to the sides.*

In Competition

Competition gymnasts are expected to start each flight phase with their legs and toes extended, and to use a continuous arm swing. Straight jumping with a continuous arm swing allows them to gain height. The height gives them time to perform complicated skills while in the air.

Body Shapes

Three basic body shapes are used in trampolining flight phase: straight body, tucked body, and piked body.

Claire Wright

Date of birth: August 5th, 1979

Nationality: British

Claire had the perfect background for a gymnast: her mother and father both coached gymnastics to children. In fact, she attended her first coaching course when she was just seven days old, and says that she's been to the gym just about every day since.

Claire's parents coached artistic gymnastics, but Claire decided that she wanted to be a trampoline gymnast. She soon became one of the best around. By the age of 13 she was in the senior national trampoline team. Her later achievements include:

- British champion 2001–2007.
- Multiple wins in the World Cup Synchronized Trampoline competition.
- Further wins in the World Cup individual competition.

3 *As the trampolinist takes off, her arms come through in front, ready to extend straight upward again, adding power to the takeoff.*

Flight 2—Tucked and Piked

Tucked, piked, and straddle-pike jumps are together known as shaped jumps. These shaped jumps are the basis of every trampolining routine.

Takeoff and Landing

Trampolinists aim to start and finish shaped jumps in the same way as a straight jump. In competition, this is what the judges want to see:

1) The trampolinist takes off with a straight body shape, arms stretched straight up.

2) Then he or she moves quickly into the shape so that it is clearly formed at the top of their flight.

3) Next the trampolinist comes out of the shape as fast as possible, so that he or she can be in a straight shape again before landing.

1 *The trampolinist takes off, ready to form a simple tuck-shaped jump. She is not going to somersault, just form a tuck.*

2 *In a tucked body shape, the trampolinist's legs are together, fully bent at the hips and knees. His/her ankles, feet, and toes are pointed, and her hands grip the shins.*

3 *In competition, the gymnast lands with her arms by her side, as part of the continuous arm swing.*

The piked body shape has feet and legs together, feet and toes pointed, and the trampolinist's legs straight. She bends deeply at the hips and extends her hands toward her feet.

The piked-straddle shape is the same as the pike, but with the legs spread. The feet must be at least shoulder-width apart, but ideally the legs should be at an angle of 90° or more, seen from above. The straddle pike must not be used for somersaults.

Basic Tucked Jump

The basic tucked jump is shown in the photo sequence. This is probably the easiest shape to learn, but is tricky to get exactly right. The shin grip is especially important: it is needed when performing somersaults, and competition judges will deduct points if the grip is not done correctly.

Basic Piked Jump

You need to be very flexible to achieve the basic piked shape. Even young, flexible trampolinists should warm up carefully before going into a piked jump. The judging standard for the piked shape is the same as in diving. This is just one of the similarities between diving and trampolining. In fact, many divers use trampolines for practice.

Putting a Routine Together

Once trampolinists can do shaped jumps, and can add somersaults and spins, they can begin to link the jumps together into a routine. This is one of the trickiest things to learn: keeping a good, steady bounce while seamlessly going from one skill to the next.

Flight 3—Adding Rotation

Rotation is the name given to the sideways twists and head-over-heels spins that trampolinists perform during their routines. When combined with the different body shapes, this results in a variety of techniques that can be bewildering to a beginner.

Adding Twist

Twist is the first rotation many beginners learn to add to their jumps. Very little power is needed is do a twist in the air: most people can manage a half twist jumping up from the floor, without even needing a trampoline.

Shape and Speed

Adding half and full twists to trampolining jumps teaches trampolinists that the shape they make in the air will affect the speed of their rotation. A long, narrow shape (the straight body position) twists quickly. A short, wide shape (the tucked body position) will twist more slowly. As the routines get more complicated, this becomes increasingly important—a slow twist requires a higher jump, to give more time to complete the twist.

Irina Karavaeva

Date of birth: May 18th, 1975

Nationality: Russian

Irina Karavaeva is arguably the best-ever female trampolinist. For example, she has won 19 World Cup contests, and no one else has yet won more than six.

Irina won the firstwomen's trampolining Olympic gold medal ever in 2000, but may be more famous because of her sense of fair play. At the 2001 world championships, a judging mistake meant that she was awarded the gold medal instead of Ana Dogonadze of Germany. Irina later gave the gold to Ana and took the silver herself. She was later given an International Fair Play Award by the International Olympic Committee as a result. Her other awards include:

- **Five times World Individual Trampoline champion (in 1994, 1998, 1999, 2005, and 2007).**
- **Five times winner of the World Cup championship (in 1997, 1999, 2000, 2002, and 2004).**

Irina Karavaeva in the finals of the world championships at Eindhoven, the Netherlands. Just as so many time before, she won and became world champion.

1 Neutral position
2 Takeoff: note the straight body shape.
3 Three-quarters of the way through the full twist.
4 Landing, still in a straight body shape.

Which Way to Twist?

The judges won't mind whether you twist to the left or the right, as long as you do it properly. The photo on the right shows a way of working out which twist direction is more comfortable for you. Once you know this, learn all twisting techniques going in that direction.

This gymnast is working out which side he feels most comfortable to twist toward. Starting from a back landing (see page 23), he does a half twist to the right, then the left. Repeating this a few times will make it clear which feels right.

Landing Skills

Not all jumps end with the trampolinist landing on his or her feet. Some end on the front, hands and knees, or back and seat. Once a trampolinist starts linking together several jumps in a row, he or she has to get used to landing and taking off from these positions.

Rotation

Practicing these landings requires the trampolinist to add either forward or backward rotation. It is important not to add too much rotation. Once your feet have left the mat, the amount of rotation is fixed until landing. Taking off with too much enthusiasm means you over-rotate and will not make a smooth landing.

A Seat Landing

1 *Takeoff for a seat landing. Notice how the trampolinist's body is angled very slightly backward—this will give her a tiny amount of rotation, ready for the change to a seated landing position.*

2 *Flight phase: the trampolinist's body remains in the straight position, with rotation slightly increased. She is aiming to land with her seat on the center cross of the bed.*

3 *As the trampolinist is just about to land, she brings her legs up (still straight) so that they land flat on the bed. At the same time, her hands land on the bed. They are just behind and to the side of the hips, with the fingers pointing forward.*

A Hands-and-Knees Landing

For a hands-and-knees landing, the trampolinist takes off with slight front rotation. She aims to land with 90° angles at the armpits, facing forward, and with a straight back.

A Back Landing

A back landing requires slight backward rotation. Judges expect the head to touch the bed at the same time as the back, and the back to be flat—looking straight up at the roof should give the right shape. The arms and legs should point straight up in the air.

A Front Landing

The front landing also requires slight front rotation. As the trampolinist lands, she pushes her feet back, landing flat on the bed from knees to chest. Her arms are in a diamond shape, with the forearms and hands flat on the bed.

Adding Shape and Somersaults

For more advanced routines, trampolinists add shape—a pike or tuck—to the flight phase. They may also increase the amount of rotation in order to do somersaults.

Adding extra rotation to a front landing (which is actually a quarter-somersault), for example, will allow a trampolinist to move to a simple full somersault.

Intermediate and Advanced

Intermediate and advanced techniques include the front somersault, which has a tucked shape; and the back somersault, where the body is kept straight. Trampolinists combine these with half and full twists in their competition routines.

Combining Skills

The best trampolinists can link together jumps that combine twists with somersaults in a long sequence of tricky techniques. They do this without losing their jumping rhythm or height. These are some of the most common jumps:

- Crash Dive: a three-quarter front somersault to land on the back.
- Lazy Back: a three-quarter back somersault to land on the front.
- Barani: a single front somersault with a half-twist.
- Rudi: a single front somersault with one-and-a-half twists.
- Randi: a single front somersault with two-and-a-half twists.
- Adolf: a single front somersault with three-and-a-half twists.
- Full Back: a full twisting single back somersault (usually done straight).
- Ball-Out: a one-and-a-quarter forward somersault done from a back landing to feet.
- Cody: a one-and-a-quarter backward somersault done from a front drop position.
- One and Three: a one-and-three-quarter front somersault (landing on the back).
- Half-Out: a double front somersault with a half-twist at the end.

No one starts off performing trampolining skills like this. It takes years of practice to build up to spectacular techniques that will wow the judges.

If you think mastering the skills of trampolining looks tricky, how about synchronized trampolining, where two gymnasts have to stay in perfect time with each other?

The Language of Trampolining

As the list on page 24 shows, trampolining has its own language. Some moves are named after the people who first made them popular. The "Barani," for example, is named after the Italian circus performer and tumbler, Alfonso Barani, who made it popular in about 1881. A side somersault, starting and finishing on the stomach, is often called a turntable. But it used to be called a Bluch, after Jim Blutch, who first made it popular in the 1940s. Many of these old names are no longer officially recognized, but are still in use in gyms and trampoline clubs around the world.

World Record Bouncing

In 1986, a six-man team from Cleveland State University set a Guinness World Record of 53 days' continuous bouncing on a trampoline.

Competitions

There are all kinds of trampoline competitions, ranging from contests between members of your local club to the world championships and the Olympic Games.

Scoring

Trampolining competitions are based on scores given by judges and the difficulty of the routine. Each routine gets two scores. The first is for difficulty, the second for the artistic quality of the performance. Every technique the trampolinist performs has a "difficulty rating," which is added to the scores given by the judges. This is a way of encouraging the gymnasts to include more difficult techniques in their routines. If they perform a hard technique with a higher skill rating perfectly, they get a higher score than they do for performing a simple technique perfectly.

Emmanuel Durand

Date of birth: June 11th, 1977

Nationality: French

In trampolining, Emmanuel Durand is best known as the former world record holder for the compulsory routine. He set a record score of 29.5 points at the 1996 world championships. But Emmanuel is famous far outside the world of trampolining. He is now putting his acrobatic training to good use as the coach of the Cirque du Soleil show in Las Vegas.

Emmanuel's other trampolining achievements include:

- **Winning world championships individual silver medal in 1996, and bronze in 1998.**
- **Winning the European championships synchronized trampoline gold medal in 1997, and world championships in 1998.**

Competition Format

At top-level competitions such as the Olympic Games, each competitor performs two routines. Each routine is made up of 10 moves. The first routine contains techniques that each trampolinist in the contest has to include. The second routine features techniques chosen by the trampolinist and his or her coach.

The judges watch closely as Germany's bronze medallist Henrik Stehlik performs during the Athens 2004 Olympic Games.

Action from the British Trampoline Championships, with two synchro trampolinists aiming for victory.

In synchronized trampoline competitions, two trampolinists use one trampoline each. They perform identical 10-move routines, aiming to keep in perfect time with each other all the way through.

Carnival Competition

Trampolining has always been closely linked to diving, because many of the skills are similar. The UK's first open trampoline competition was part of a water carnival held by Ilford Diving Club in 1957.

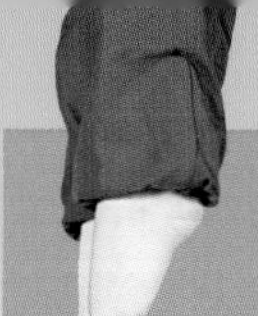

World & Olympic Champions

Individual Trampoline World Champions

Year	Held	Women	Country	Men	Country
2008	Portugal	Karen Cockburn	Canada	Dong Dong	China
2007	Canada	Irina Karavaeva	Russia	Shuai Yi	China
2005	Netherlands	Irina Karavaeva	Russia	A. Rusakov	Russia
2003	Germany	Karen Cockburn	Canada	Henrik Stehik	Germany
2001	Denmark	Anna Dogonadze	Georgia	A. Moskalenko	Russia
1999	South Africa	Irina Karavaeva	Russia	A. Moskalenko	Russia
1998	Australia	Irina Karavaeva	Russia	G. Khnychev	Russia
1996	Canada	Tatiana Kovaleva	Russia	Dmitri Poliaroush	Belarus
1994	Portugal	Irina Karavaeva	Russia	A. Moskalenko	Russia
1992	New Zealand	Elena Merkulova	Russia	A. Moskalenko	Russia
1990	Germany	Elena Merkulova	USSR	A. Moskalenko	USSR
1988	USA	R. Khoperia	USSR	V. Krasnochapka	USSR
1986	France	Tatiana Lushina	USSR	Lionel Pioline	France
1984	Japan	Susan Shotton	UK	Lionel Pioline	France
1982	USA	Ruth Keller	Switzerland	Carl Furrer	UK
1980	Switzerland	Ruth Keller	Switzerland	S. Matthews	UK
1978	Australia	T. Anisimova	USSR	Evgeni Janes	USSR
1976	USA	S. Levina	USSR	Evgeni Janes	USSR
1974	South Africa	A. Nicholson	USA	Richard Tison	France
1972	Germany	A. Nicholson	USA	Paul Luxon	UK
1970	Switzerland	Renee Ransom	USA	Wayne Miller	USA
1968	Netherlands	Judy Wills Cline	USA	David Jacobs	USA
1967	UK	Judy Wills Cline	USA	David Jacobs	USA
1966	USA	Judy Wills Cline	USA	Wayne Miller	USA
1965	UK	Judy Wills Cline	USA	Gary Erwin	USA

Olympic Champions

Year	Held	Women	Country	Men	Country
2008	China	He Wenna	China	Lu Chunlong	China
2004	Greece	Anna Dogonadze	Georgia	Yuri Nikitin	Ukraine
2000	Australia	Irina Karavaeva	Russia	Alexander Moskalenko	Russia

Glossary and Websites

Bossaball A sport mixing volleyball and trampolining, which allows the competitors to leap to great heights before knocking the ball over the net at the opposition

Coordination Skillful movement of different parts of the body at the same time. Gymnastics in general, including trampolining, requires excellent coordination.

Flexible Able to bend the joints of the body easily and a long way.

Pike A body shape with: feet and legs together; feet and toes pointed; legs straight; deep bend at the hips; extended hands toward feet, and elbows kept bent.

Rotation A turn or spin along a central axis (an axis is an imaginary straight line around which something spins). In trampolining, rotations are either spins or somersaults.

Slamball A version of basketball with four trampoline beds near each net, allowing spectacular slam dunks and defensive moves.

Slam-dunk A basketball move in which the player leaps high into the air and bangs the ball down through the scoring hoop.

Somersault A head-over-heels rotation.

Spike A volleyball move in which a player jumps high in the air in order to smash the ball down into the opposition's court.

Synchronized trampoline An event for two trampolinists, each with their own trampoline, who try to perform a side-by-side routine in which they exactly mirror each other's movements.

Trapeze artists Acrobatic circus performers who swing between trapeze (trapeze are short poles hanging from two cables, one at each end of the pole). The performers do spectacular rotations, similar to some trampoline moves, as they swap from one trapeze to the other.

Tuck A body shape with: legs together, fully bent at the hips and knees; ankles, feet, and toes pointed; and hands gripping the shins.

Tumbler An acrobatic performer who does spectacular jumps, with lots of rotations, after a fast run-up.

Twist A turning-to-the-side rotation.

Webbed fabric Fabric made by weaving together strips of material.

Websites

www.en.beijing2008.cn/
This is part of the Beijing Olympic website. Click on Trampoline to find information about the sport's Olympic history, an explanation of some of the technical terms, clothing and equipment, and the Olympic trampoline events.

www.fig-gymnastics.com
The home page of the Fédération Internationale de Gymnastique, the world governing body for gymnastics. One section of the site is about trampolining, and allows you to keep up with competition results and other news from the sport.

http://www.usta1.org
The home U.S. Tumbling & Trampoline Association, started in 1971. Here you can learn about officers, awards, scholarships, general rules for tumbling, trampoline, and double-mini. Also check this website for a calendar of events and information about members and competitiors.

Note to parents and teachers: every effort has been made by the Publishers to ensure that these websites are suitable for children, that they are of the highest educational value, and that they contain no inappropriate or offensive material. However, because of the nature of the Internet, it is impossible to guarantee that the contents of these sites will not be altered. We strongly advise that Internet access be supervised by a responsible adult.

Index